"Hi, my name is _____, and I am your group facilitator tonight."

Welcome

We welcome you to the meeting of Phobics Anonymous. We are a group of people suffering, recovering and freed from irrational fears, phobias and panic attacks. We are here to share our experience, strength and hope. Accept what you like and leave the rest.

Through following The Twelve Steps of Phobics Anonymous, we are on a journey to wholeness, wellness, and a life based on faith not fear.

We are pleased you are here. We ask that you come here with an open mind and a willingness. Take what you want from our group dialogue and leave the rest. Please respect the confidentiality and anonymity of what's said in this room as we share and grow together in the Spirit.

Would someone please read:
1. Opening Prayer
2. Description
3. The Twelve Steps
4. The Twelve Traditions
5. Meeting Guidelines

_____
Fill in meeting day and time

Opening Prayer

Our Father, we come to You as a friend.

You have said that where two or three are gathered in Your name, there You will be in the midst.

We believe You are with us now. We believe this is something You would have us do, and that it has Your blessing.

We believe that You want us to be real partners with You in this business of living, accepting our full responsibility, and certain that the rewards will be freedom, growth and happiness.

For this we are grateful.
We ask You at all times to guide us according to Your will.

Description Of The Phobic

Who Is A Phobic?

We are a group of individuals who found that we are powerless over fear. We experience irrational fears often accompanied by acute anxiety and panic attacks. At times we experienced physical symptoms to such an extent that they made our lives unmanageable.

Our fear of fear - of being trapped in our emotions, made us feel we were either going crazy, going to lose control, or die. The perimeter of our world became smaller and smaller as we avoided situations, people and places; such as markets, restaurants, theaters, social functions, driving, job related activities, etc.

We sought help from physicians, psychologists, psychiatrists, hypnotherapists, nutritionists, family and friends. Many of us self-medicated with alcohol and drugs. All of these provided temporary relief. They addressed the physical, emotional and intellectual part of man. Yet, there was a missing link. We found the recovery process was incomplete without addressing the spiritual aspect of man.

The Twelve Steps of Phobics Anonymous

1. We admitted we were powerless over fear and that our lives had become unmanageable.

2. We came to believe that a power greater than ourselves could restore us to sanity.

3. We made a decision to turn our will and our lives over to the care of God, as we understand Him.

4. We made a searching and fearless moral inventory of ourselves.

5. We admitted to God, to ourselves, and to another human being the exact nature of our wrongs.

6. We became ready to have God, as we understood Him, remove our defects of character.

7. We humbly asked Him to remove our shortcomings.

8. We made a list of all persons we had harmed and became willing to make amends to them all.

9. We made direct amends to such people whenever possible except when to do so would injure them or others.

10. We continued to take a daily inventory and when we were wrong, promptly admitted it.

11. We sought through prayer and meditation to improve our conscious contact with God, as we understood him, praying only for knowledge of His will for us and the power to carry it out.

12. Having had a spiritual awakening as a result of these steps, we sought to carry the message to others and to practice its principles in all our affairs.

The Twelve Traditions of Phobics Anonymous

1. Our common welfare should come first; personal recovery depends upon PA unity.

2. For our group purpose there is but one ultimate authority- a loving God as He may express Himself in our group conscience. Our leaders are but trusted servants, they do not govern.

3. The only requirement for membership is a desire to recover from phobias and panic attacks.

4. Each group should be autonomous except in matters affecting other groups or PA as a whole.

5. Each group has but one primary purpose-to carry the message to the phobic who still suffers.

6. A PA group ought never endorse, finance, or lend the PA name to any related facility or outside enterprise, lest problems of money, property or prestige divert us from our primary spiritual purpose.

7. Every PA group ought to be fully self-supporting, declining outside contributions.

8. Phobics Anonymous should remain forever nonprofessional, but our service centers may employ special workers.

9. PA, as such, ought never be organized, but may create service boards or committees directly responsible to those they serve.

10. Phobics Anonymous has no opinion on outside issues; hence the PA name ought never be drawn into public controversy.

11. Our public relations policy is based on attraction rather than promotion; we need always maintain personal anonymity at the level of press, radio, and films.

12. Anonymity is the spiritual foundation of all our Traditions, ever reminding us to place principles before personalities.

The Promises

- Recovery is an ongoing daily process which requires commitment and dedication leading to continuous progress and growth.

- We will be amazed before we are half-way through.

- We are going to experience a feeling of freedom and newly found happiness.

- We will not regret the past nor wish to shut the door on it but will use our painful experience as a stepping stone for growth.

- We will comprehend the word serenity, and we will experience calmness and freedom from fear.

- No matter how high on the anxiety scale our fear has peaked, we will see how our experience can benefit others, and in helping them we will aid our own recovery.

- We will no longer fear nor be anxious about how others respond to our feelings. Our need to be perfect and people-pleasers will diminish.

- We will no longer fear rejections nor being hurt by others.

- We will no longer respond in fear to other peoples' actions and attitudes.

- What we say and how we act will no longer be determined by our fear of others' feelings.

- We will no longer have difficulty expressing our feelings.

- Our serenity will no longer be determined by how others are feeling or behaving.

- The feelings of uselessness, rejection, abandonment, and self-pity will disappear.

- We will no longer be the nucleus of our own world but will gain an interest and understanding of our fellow phobics.

- Our self-will and compulsion for control will leave us.

- Our catastrophic and negative thinking as well as our attitudes will change.

- Fear of people, places, things, and situations will be replaced by faith.

- We will learn how to accept, cope with, and float through situations which previously panicked us.

- We will come to accept our Higher Power and realize our Higher Power is doing for us what we could not do for ourselves.

- We will gain the inner direction to stand and face our fears rather than retreat.

- Our shame, bondage, and self-made prison walls will crumble.

Notes for Leader

This section will present a format for conducting a Phobics Anonymous meeting. We have found one or two hours is an adequate length of time for constructive interaction. Meetings should be held at least once a week if possible. The meeting has a leader who is a member of the group. Each week leadership changes on a voluntary basis.

Refreshments can be available and members receive a telephone list to use for ongoing support contact. Phobics Anonymous literature is displayed.

The facilitator asks each person to introduce themselves by first name only.

Facilitator then shares their own experience, strength and hope for approximately 5 minutes.

After that the group is invited to share individually.

The facilitator picks a question and each participant shares if he/she desires.

Newcomers are encouraged to share whenever needed but there are no requirements to share.

A basket is passed for a voluntary donation for use of the meeting room.

A sign up sheet or calendar is passed for first names and phone numbers for calling between meetings.

Closing:

The facilitator asks someone to close with the Lord's Prayer.

Facilitator reminds the group that whatever is shared should stay within these walls. We ask you to respect the confidentiality and anonymity of each member. A sign up sheet is passed for those who would like to facilitate a meeting.

If you agree or don't agree with what is shared, be sure to take what you like and leave the rest.

Various types of 12 Step Meetings

1. Choose a step.
2. Choose a topic from a step: honesty, surrender, powerlessness etc.
3. Do a 4th step inventory topic.
4. Have a speaker meeting.
5. Read a page from 12 steps of Phobic Anonymous and discuss it.

Meeting Guidelines

1. There are no requirements to speak, share or read at a meeting.

2. All participation is totally voluntary. You are welcome to just listen if you desire.

3. All sharing is strictly confidential and kept within the walls of our meeting.

4. Limit your sharing to a couple of minutes, giving all a chance to participate.

5. Do not cross talk during sharing.

6. Do not accentuate symptoms but refer to levels of anxiety from 1 to 10—one being the least and 10 being the highest.

7. Accentuate the positive when possible.

8. Feel free to sit where you want and to leave the room when you want.

9. When facilitating begin and end the meeting on time.

10. There are no costs or fees and all donations are voluntary.

11. Use the meeting list of names and numbers for extra support between meetings.

Questions for PA Step Study

Step 1

1. In what ways am I powerless over my fears and panic reactions?
2. How has fear affected my life?
3. In what ways is my life unmanageable?

Step 2

1. How has my health or wholeness or sanity been affected by my irrational fears and panic attacks?
2. What beliefs have I held that may have contributed to my anxiety?
3. Do I believe or can I come to believe in a power greater than myself? How can I grow in my belief?

Step 3

1. In what ways will surrendering my life and will to a Higher Power relieve me of the burden of anxiety and fear?
2. What results have I had from my attempts to control my fears and to control other people?
3. Can I give up trying to control and let my Higher Power be in control?
4. How difficult is giving up my will to a Higher Power's will for me?

Step 4

1. What moral compromises or dishonesties could have affected my peace of mind? What areas do I try to hide from others?
2. What things in my life could I be in denial about? Why is it so difficult for me to face reality in regard to those things?
3. How has my fear of rejection or abandonment influenced my behavior?
4. Has the area of sexual relations played a destructive role in my life and lead to fears? Looking at my sexual relations, what could I do to eliminate my fears?

Step 5

1. How can confessing our wrongs lessen our fears?
2. By bringing my wrongs into the light, are my fears being alleviated?
3. Do I find relief in not having to hide my wrongs? Am I growing spiritually?
4. In what ways do a lot of guilt and shame affect me?

Step 6.

1. How does humility help me become more ready to have my defects of character removed?

Step 7

1. Am I able to surrender my shortcomings to God and let him help me?
2. How do I still try to do my Higher Power's job by trying to control my fears, circumstances or others?

Step 8

1. Am I afraid to make amends to the people I've hurt? Why?
2. How can I forgive others who have hurt me and let go of past hurts?

Step 9

1. What are some ways I can make direct amends to the people I have hurt?
2. Do I find reconciliation and restoration bring me peace and healing? When these attempts are refused, can I surrender the situation to God?

Step 10

1. Do I take personal responsibility for my own behavior? How?
2. How possible is it for me to focus on myself instead of others? Do I blame others for my shortcomings?
3. How does evaluating myself daily help me in my spiritual growth?
4. Am I careful not to take other people's inventory?

Step 11

1. In what ways can I incorporate prayer and daily meditation into my daily schedule?
2. How does prayer and meditation help me in my recovery?

Step 12

1. How do I define a spiritual awakening, and do I seek one or have I had one?
2. Do I "walk the talk" by living the spiritual principles in addition to talking about them?
3. In what ways do I carry the message to others?

Need books?

You can order more copies of the books at amazon.com

Phobics
Anonymous

Meeting Guide

Rosemary

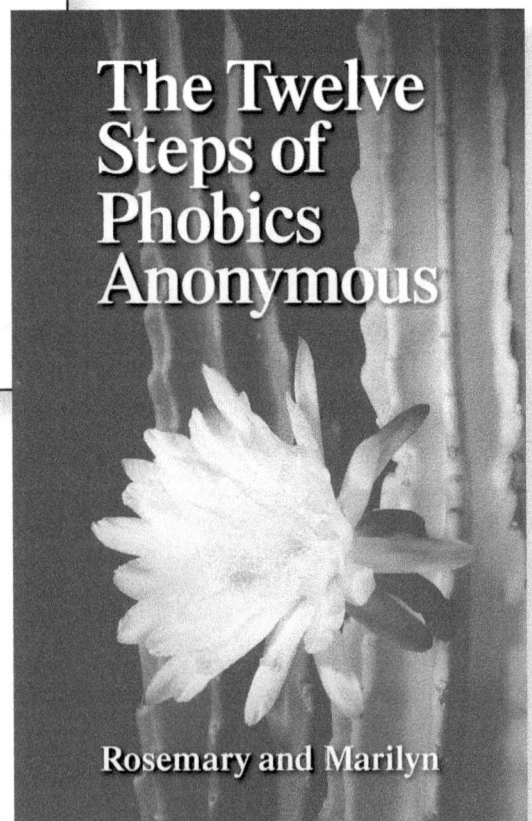

The Twelve
Steps of
Phobics
Anonymous

Rosemary and Marilyn

Closing Prayers

The Lord's Prayer

Our Father which art in heaven, hallowed be Thy name. Thy kingdom come. Thy will be done on earth as it is in heaven. Give us this day our daily bread and forgive us our trespasses, as we forgive those who trespass against us.

And lead us not into temptation, but deliver us from evil: For Thine is the kingdom and the power, and the glory, forever. Amen

The Serenity Prayer

God grant me the serenity to accept the things I cannot change, the courage to change the things I can, and the wisdom to know the difference.

If You Suffer From Panic Attacks, Phobias, Anxiety and Depression You Are Invited To Attend:

PHOBICS ANONYMOUS

A 12 Step Recovery Meeting

Dates:

Time:

Location:

Meeting Info - Call (000) 000-0000

Phobics Anonymous, 12-step Program for those with anxiety, depression, panic attacks, and phobias. Meetings held in (list location).
Information, (000) 000-0000